A-B-C DELEGATION

For permission requests, contact:
info@abcdelegation.com

This book is a work of nonfiction. Unless otherwise indicated, all names, examples, and case studies are either used with permission or are fictional and intended for illustrative purposes only.

Title: *A-B-C Delegation: The Manager's Guide to Effective Delegation*
Author: Stefan J. Feuerstein

Published by Stefan Feuerstein

ISBN Ebook: 979-8-9989460-0-4
ISBN Paperback: 979-8-9989460-9-7

First Edition
Printed in the United States of America

Design by Vanessa Mendozzi

www.abcdelegation.com

A-B-C DELEGATION

THE MANAGER'S GUIDE TO EFFECTIVE DELEGATION

STEFAN J. FEUERSTEIN

CONTENTS

Before we start…

A Tale of Two Managers

Two managers manage similar-sized teams.

Manager A wants to be involved in everything. He sits in on every call, approves all the PowerPoints of his team, and doesn't want anything to be done without his knowledge. His team always waits for his instructions and does not step up unless asked. They feel that they have no ownership of the work that they do. After all, Manager A owns it all. He is in charge.

Manager B, on the other hand, uses the **A-B-C Delegation** system. His employees know exactly what they are responsible for. They know what they can do independently, when to update him, and when to ask him for authorization before proceeding. They feel ownership, pride in their work, and have clear objectives.

Manager A works late nights. Manager B builds leaders.

Which do you want to be?

Introduction

Delegation is one of the most powerful tools in a manager's toolkit, but also one of the most misunderstood.

Some managers hold on too tightly, driven by perfectionism. Others let go too completely, only to be surprised when things veer off track. Many are simply overwhelmed, unsure how to stay connected without micromanaging.

A-B-C Delegation is a simple, visual, and actionable framework for assigning responsibility with clarity, following up without micromanaging, and empowering your team to operate at their highest level...all while keeping you aligned with the mission.

This isn't just theory. It's a field-tested system developed over two decades of leading teams ranging from two hundred employees to a few thousand, both in nonprofit organizations and private corporations. It works in high-stakes, real-world settings because it solves real problems.

Early in my leadership journey, I found myself stuck in a frustrating pattern: my meetings were full of decisions I shouldn't have been involved in; there were tasks on my desk that belonged elsewhere; and I saw that my team was unclear on where each member's ownership began and ended.

I kept thinking, *I wish I could trust my team to take initiative...without cutting me out of the loop.*

But wishing isn't leadership. Building a system is. As I searched for a solution, I soon realized that most leadership problems that I saw were really delegation problems in disguise:

Overload? I was holding too much. Drift? My team lacked clarity. Bottlenecks? I hadn't distributed responsibility. Burnout? I wasn't building enough capacity in my team.

Solving these at the root meant building a framework and cultivating a culture, not just issuing commands, and the answer I found was what I call **A-B-C Delegation.**

A-B-C Delegation resolves ambiguity, builds trust, and develops new leaders, all while providing a shared language for who owns what, and for how to stay connected.

Instead of just assigning tasks, **A-B-C Delegation** answers three critical questions:

(A). What does the employee own outright?
(B). What should they inform me about?
(C). What still requires my decision?

It's not complex. In fact, its power lies in its simplicity. But like any good system, it requires structure, follow-up, and leadership for it to produce best results.

This handbook will show you how to assign responsibility to your team in a way that is easy to manage, and it will show you how to comply with the three requirements that will make your delegation system effective and your leadership strong. It distills the lessons I learned, often the hard way, into a practical guide, and it's designed to help you lead with clarity, avoid burnout, and build teams that own the mission alongside you.

This framework changed how I lead, and how my teams have performed. I want it to do the same for you.

THE A-B-C DELEGATION FRAMEWORK

Delegation is essential for effective leadership. But without a clear framework, it can feel like a gamble or a loss of oversight. Managers often hesitate: What should I delegate? To whom? And how do I stay connected without micromanaging?

In this book, you will learn that **A-B-C Delegation** is a practical, visual system. It treats management as leadership for people working at their highest level of responsibility and authority, aligned to a shared objective. With **A-B-C Delegation,** managers stay informed and in control without becoming bottlenecks for work that doesn't need their direct attention or involvement.

Step One
THE MISSION FRAME

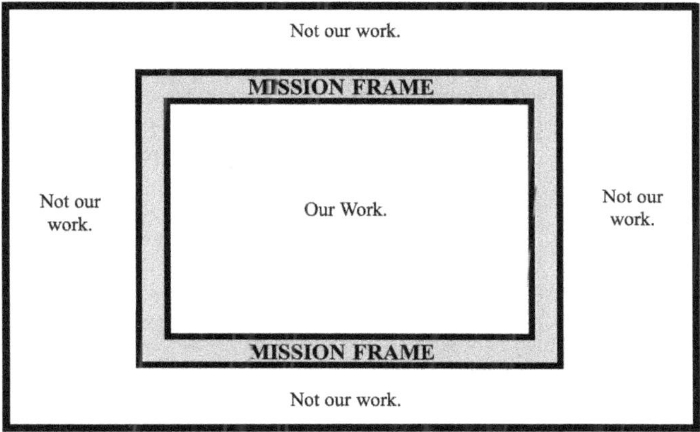

The **Mission Frame** represents the total scope of what your organization exists to do. Anything outside of it shouldn't receive time, attention, or resources.

Step Two
THE MANDATE FRAMES

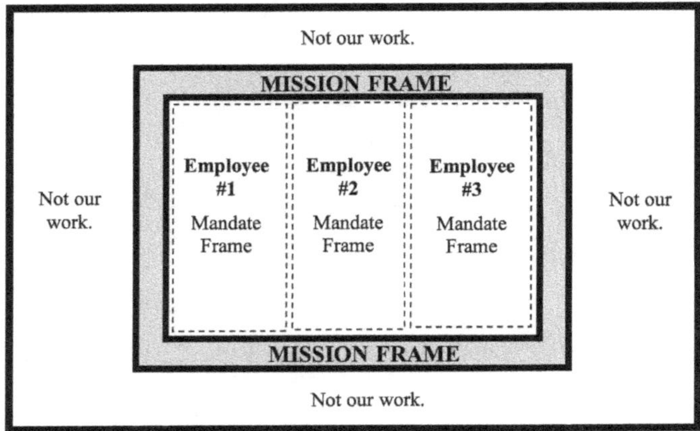

Assign the Mission Frame to your team. Each person or department receives a **Mandate Frame:** their defined area of responsibility within the organization's mission.

Mandate Frames may be broad or narrow and can sometimes overlap, but together, they should account for the full mission. Each Mandate Frame functions like a "personal mission frame" for the employee who owns it. Everything inside it is that employee's responsibility. What's outside isn't.

Step Three
THE A-B-C CATEGORIES

Divide each Mandate Frame into three categories:

A

Category A: "Do what you want."

No manager involvement needed

Typically low-risk, clearly defined duties

B

Category B: "Do what you want, but inform me."

Tasks that don't require prior approval

The manager must be kept informed after the action

C

Category C: "Ask me first."

Tasks requiring authorization before action

High-risk, high-impact, or cross-functional issues

Invest early effort in helping employees understand where each task falls. The clearer the boundaries, the less you need to be involved in daily operations. Employees can act without delay in Category A or Category B. Only Category C requires pausing for manager input.

Ensure that each level of management does this with their teams, to ensure organization-wide **A-B-C Delegation.**

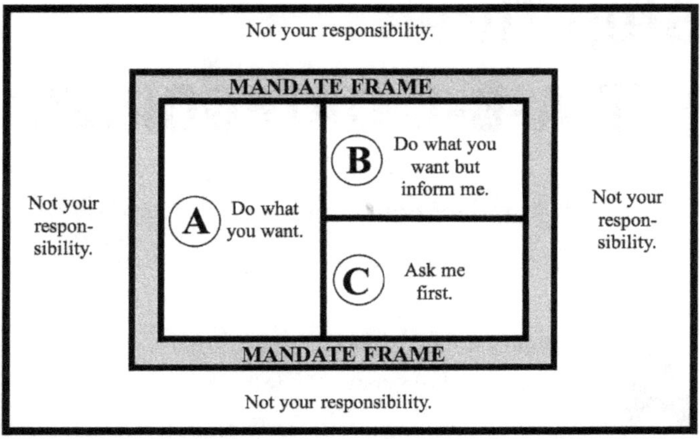

Despite its simplicity, **A-B-C Delegation** requires a manager's attention and maintenance for it to function at its best.

When applied correctly, **A-B-C Delegation** empowers employees at every level of the organization to operate at full capacity without sacrificing alignment or accountability. It's a system that builds autonomy and trust for employees of every rank in the hierarchy, while ensuring the managers are informed where it matters most.

The manager doesn't give up their ultimate responsibility. Instead, they create distributed ownership, enabling more output with less friction and bottlenecks.

The 3 Requirements for Successful A-B-C Delegation:

1 **FOLLOW UP**
A-B-C Check-ins.
Evaluation.
Stay connected.

2 **RESOLVE DESTRUCTIVE CONFLICT**
Identify it. Fix it.
Remove it if necessary.

3 **DEVELOP NEW LEADERS**
Build Capacity.
Create Opportunity.
Cultivate Responsibility.

Summary: The A-B-C Delegation Framework

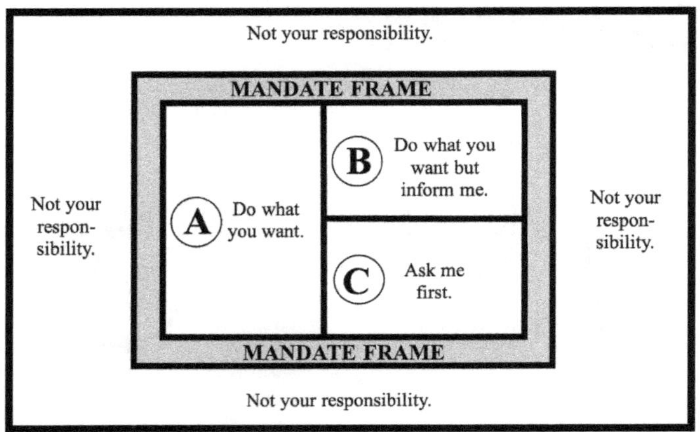

Requirements for Success

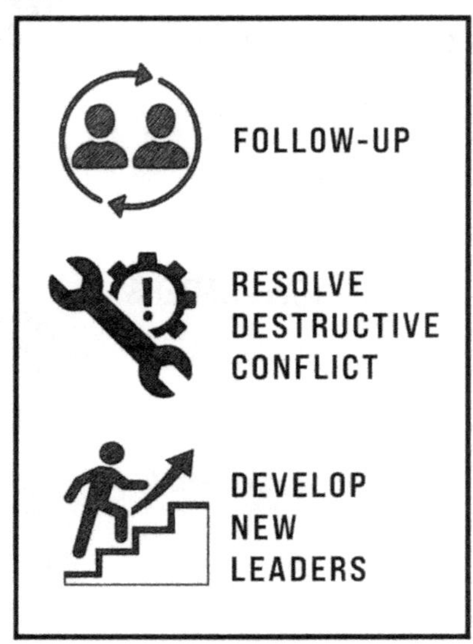

Introducing A-B-C Delegation

DO THIS TODAY

- ☐ Draw your Mission Frame. Is what your organization does perfectly clear to you? Is it also clear to you what your organization does not do?
- ☐ Determine the Mandate Frames of your direct reports. Is it clear to you who is responsible for what?
- ☐ Reflect on a recent delegation that went wrong. Was it due to lack of clarity, follow-up, or trust?
- ☐ Write down one thing you tend to hold onto too tightly. Decide how you could delegate it.
- ☐ Introduce the A-B-C concept informally in a conversation with a colleague to test understanding.
- ☐ Choose one direct report. Draft their Mandate Frame on paper and categorize their tasks into A, B, and C.

REQUIREMENT ONE:

FOLLOW UP

Two tools will allow you to FOLLOW UP with your team effectively when delegating.

1.1 – A-B-C CHECK-INS

Stay informed of what matters after delegating responsibility.

1.2 – EVALUATION

Know what/who is working, and what/who is not.

FOLLOW UP – 1.1
A-B-C Check-ins

A-B-C Delegation is not a license to disconnect or abdicate. It's a method for structured empowerment and it's a partnership across all members of the team.

You should be proud when your team steps up and takes ownership, but delegation doesn't mean you're done. You still have a role to play. After all, you are still ultimately responsible for what gets done...and for what doesn't.

It is common for employees to want to inform their managers of everything that they do. They want to show how busy they have been. But instead, implement a meeting structure and cadence that inspires ownership and gets you the information that you need without getting lost in the busyness of every day.

For new team members, schedule A-B-C Check-ins more frequently to reinforce alignment. For employees experienced in **A-B-C Delegation**, you can reduce the frequency and trust them to reach out as needed. Avoid sprawling conversations that touch everything but resolve nothing, and keep it tight and intentional by communicating this meeting format with those you will follow up with.

You may prefer to have some communication flow through emails and reports, but regular, structured check-ins are essential, especially for employees still learning the **A-B-C Delegation** system.

Most A-B-C Check-ins can be short. But short doesn't

mean unstructured or superficial. Don't let meetings spiral into long conversations about things that you, quite frankly, don't need to be involved in, but make sure you do invest time in what's important.

HOW TO DO IT:

A-B-C Check-ins – The Meeting Format

Category A – Skip it. √

These are "Do what you want" tasks. If something needs input or if you want updates, it's not Category A.

Category B – Ask for updates. √

Let employees bring you up to speed on the actions they've taken. This is your chance to spot patterns, course-correct, or offer guidance.

Category C – Provide input and approvals. √

Make the decisions only you can make, and ensure your employee has the support they need to act.

Review – Calibrate load and scope. √

Ask how the employee is managing their Mandate Frame. Are they overwhelmed? Ready for more? Facing Conflicts?

Recognition – Celebrate progress. √

A moment of praise can fuel weeks of effort.

Close. √

End with clarity: next steps, follow-ups, and alignment.

HOW TO SAY IT:

A-B-C Check-ins

Starter Lines: Use these to set tone and expectations at the start of the check-in:

- "Let's keep this short and focused so we both get back to work quickly."
- "I want you to come ready with any Category B updates and any Category C issues you need my input on."
- "These check-ins are about supporting your ownership, not controlling your work."

1. Mentoring Approach

Supportive, growth-focused

- "I appreciate the initiative you're taking. Use these check-ins to bring anything you're unsure about."
- "Don't feel you need to have everything perfect. This is a space to work through things together."
- "If something feels unclear, I want you to feel confident bringing it up."

2. Firm Approach
Direct, clear expectations

- "Let's go through this by category, starting with B. What should I be informed about?"
- "Category C items always need to come to me first. That's not negotiable."
- "How are you doing with the overall workload in your Mandate Frame? Anything feeling off-scope or heavy? Any conflicts?"

3. Tough Approach
Accountability-driven, corrective tone

- "If you're not bringing Category C issues to me before acting, that's a breakdown in the system. That can't happen."
- "You need to be prepared. These check-ins aren't just updates. They're part of how we stay aligned."
- "If something is in Category B or C and you don't raise it, I see that as avoidance, not ownership."

Closing Lines: Wrap up with clarity and direction:

- "Great, we're aligned. Let me know if anything shifts before our next check-in."
- "Thanks. You're doing well. Keep ownership strong, and keep me in the loop."

- "We'll continue weekly check-ins until we see consistent alignment, then adjust frequency."

Takeaway: A-B-C Check-ins should be short, structured, and purposeful. Use tone intentionally to match the situation. Be mentoring when guiding, firm when setting structure, tough when accountability is at stake.

Example:

A-B-C Check-ins

Characters:

- Morgan (Manager, Director of Guest Experience)
- Luis (Employee, Front Desk Operations Lead)

Mandate Frame Overview:

- **Category A:** Guest check-ins, inquiries, shift scheduling
- **Category B:** Upgrades, minor guest compensation, recurring maintenance
- **Category C:** Staff reassignment, major compensation, escalated VIP issues

Check-In Conversation:

Morgan: "Thanks for making time. Let's keep this short. What Category B updates should I know about?"

Luis: "I comped a late checkout and champagne for a couple with a noise complaint, and they left happy. Also, room 304 had another ceiling leak. Third time this month."

Morgan: "Good call on the guest experience. I'll follow up on 304 with facilities. Anything in Category C?"

Luis: "A VIP guest returns next week. They had issues last time. I have ideas but want your input."

Morgan: "Let's talk through it after this. One more thing: how are you holding up with coverage?"

Luis: "Weekends are tight. Late check-ins pile up."

Morgan: "We'll adjust shifts or add a flex person. And I appreciate how steady things have been lately. Keep it up."

Luis: "Thanks, that means a lot."

Morgan: "Great. Let's stay on this schedule."

Why It Worked:

- Morgan skips Category A. He trusts the system.
- Focuses on key Category B and C items.
- Checks alignment on workload.
- Delivers specific recognition.

Takeaway: Short, structured check-ins strengthen clarity, reinforce the A-B-C system, and build trust without micromanagement.

FOLLOW UP – 1.2 Evaluation

A-B-C Delegation isn't a "set it and forget it" model. To ensure it works, managers must build in structured evaluation that supports accountability and growth without micromanaging. When done right, evaluation boosts performance, strengthens trust, and reinforces responsibility.

You may already have an effective evaluation system. If so, that's fine. Just make sure that the delegation-related elements outlined in this chapter are added to it. If you don't yet have an effective evaluation system, invest time and resources into developing one. Remember that work without evaluation is not strategic. You can't measure your progress toward your goals if you don't evaluate.

Set the Right Tone

Evaluation should not feel like punishment. It's a tool for growth. Employees need to hear: "You're not expected to be perfect. You're expected to grow, and I'm here to support that."

Be transparent by letting your team know when and how evaluations will happen. Surprise inspections can be useful, but they should complement a consistent evaluation system, not replace it.

Avoid the trap of being a "Shadow Manager." Don't act on gossip or snoop for faults. This creates suspicion and erodes trust. Instead, evaluate openly and professionally.

Five Core Components of Effective Evaluation

1. Performance

Be sure to measure what matters. Is the work in each A, B, and C category being done well? Tie metrics to the mission, and avoid tracking busyness instead of impact. An evaluation system based on the wrong metrics is pointless.

Ask:

- Does this activity advance our goals?
- Are we measuring meaningful progress?

2. Judgment

Can your team distinguish correctly between Categories A, B, and C? Misclassification shows a gap in understanding and weakens the delegation system.

When employees handle judgment well, recognize it. When they don't, correct it. Reinforce that ownership includes knowing when to act, inform, or escalate.

3. Communication

Effective communication is timely, relevant, and honest. Evaluate if team members:

- Share what matters, when it matters.
- Communicate openly, even when it's uncomfortable.
- Stay professional and mission-focused.

Strong communication supports alignment and teamwork, so evaluate it intentionally.

4. Proactivity

Does your team anticipate problems and opportunities, or just react? Proactivity shows deep ownership, so build a culture that values foresight.

Ask:

- "What challenges do you see coming?"
- "How are we preparing for future changes?"

5. Leadership

Are your people growing into leaders? Evaluate whether they:

- Model your organization's values.
- Empower their own teams.
- Develop others through **A-B-C Delegation.**

Don't reward managers who hoard control. Remind them that true leadership builds other leaders. And do not ignore toxic behavior that runs contrary to your institutional values, even when the numbers look good.

Act on the Results

Evaluation without action is just paperwork. A strong evaluation system means nothing without action. Use what you learn to:

- Recognize top performers
- Coach underperformers
- Clarify expectations
- Reassign or remove if necessary

Reward professional growth, not just results, so that you can inspire a culture of continuous improvement.

Evaluation reinforces **A-B-C Delegation** by keeping everyone aligned, accountable, and growing. Focus on performance, judgment, communication, proactivity, and leadership, and deliver feedback with clarity. Act on the insights that you gain, and always aim to build trust and ownership.

You don't need to watch everything. You need to watch what matters...and act on it.

HOW TO SAY IT:

Evaluation

Starter Lines: Open the conversation with clarity and intent:

- "Let's use this time to reflect, not just review. I want to understand what's working and where we can grow."
- "This isn't a judgment meeting. It's a growth check-in. And growth includes feedback."
- "We're going to walk through performance, communication, and judgment using the A-B-C framework."

1. Mentoring Approach

Supportive, development-focused

- "You're showing real effort, and I want to make sure that effort translates into strong outcomes."
- "Let's look at what went well and where we can strengthen things together."
- "You don't have to have it all figured out. I'm here to help you grow through this."

2. Firm Approach

Clear, performance-aligned tone

- "This should have been treated as a Category C task. I want to understand what led you to treat it as Category B."
- "Let's realign on expectations. Going forward, I need immediate visibility on issues like this."
- "You're responsible for your Mandate Frame. Part of that is flagging concerns before they become problems."

3. Tough Approach

High-accountability, corrective tone

- "This level of judgment isn't acceptable. We've discussed it before, and now I need to see a change."
- "Silence isn't success. If you're not flagging Category C issues, you're exposing the team and the mission."
- "I can coach performance. But if communication continues to break down, we'll need to reevaluate your role."

Closing Lines: End with clear next steps and support:

- "Here's what I expect moving forward: weekly check-ins and prompt communication about Category C issues."

- "This is a reset, not a reprimand. Let's make this the point where things turn around."
- "You're capable. Now let's prove it through consistent execution and proactive communication."

Takeaway: Evaluation conversations should reinforce trust, not fear. Use mentoring to encourage, firmness to clarify, and toughness to correct. Always tie feedback to ownership and the A-B-C framework.

Example:

Effective Evaluation

Characters:

- Jim (Director of Finance)
- Rhea (Finance Associate)

Mandate Frame:

- **Category A:** Expense reconciliation, reimbursements
- **Category B**: Budget drafts, variance tracking
- **Category C:** Final board reports, grant reallocations

What Went Wrong:

Rhea worked independently but without structure. Jim, overwhelmed, skipped check-ins and evaluations. Errors built up unnoticed: misclassified payments, premature decisions, lack of updates. Leadership received flawed reports, and donors raised concerns.

The Conversation:

Jim: "Rhea, I know you've been working hard, and that effort matters. But we need to talk about recent reporting issues. They've had real consequences."

Rhea: "I didn't realize things were off. I thought I was doing the right thing and didn't want to slow things down."

Jim: "That's fair. But I didn't support you properly. I never set up consistent evaluations. We both need to adjust."

Rhea: "I think I got overconfident. And maybe I misunderstood what counted as Category C."

Jim: "Exactly. So here's what we'll do: clarify categories, schedule weekly check-ins, and implement a monthly evaluation system. This isn't punishment. Iit's structure to support your growth."

Why It Worked:

- Jim owns the gap in oversight
- Rhea is held accountable with respect
- The A-B-C framework is reinforced, not abandoned
- Clear structure replaces guesswork

Takeaway: Evaluation isn't about blame. It's about alignment. When feedback is consistent, clear, and actionable, it becomes a tool for growth and trust.

Summary: Following Up

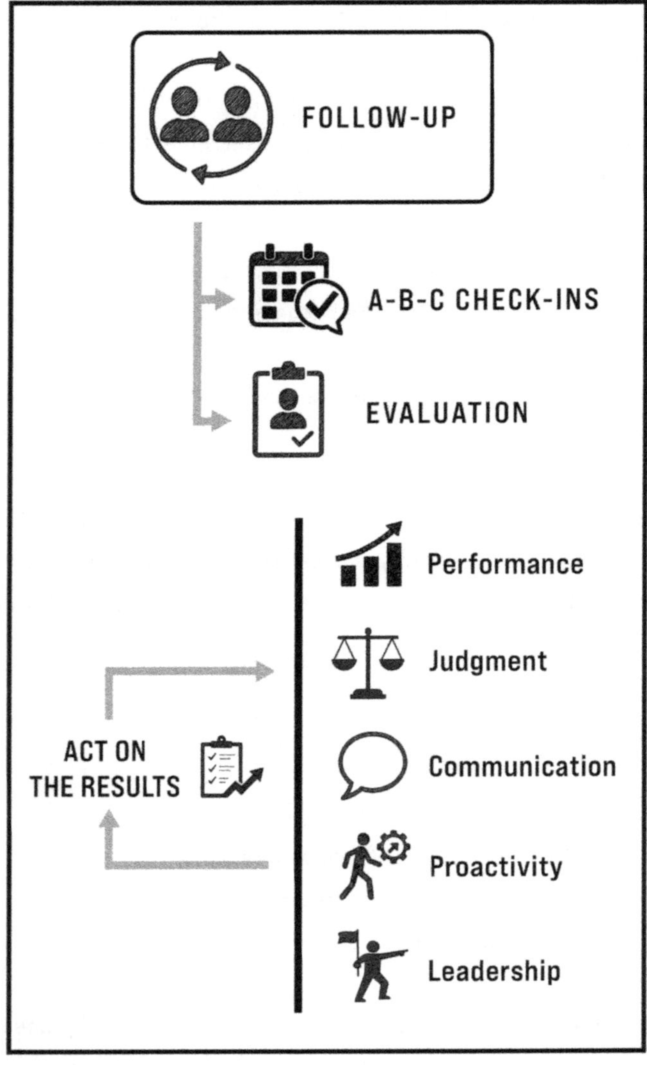

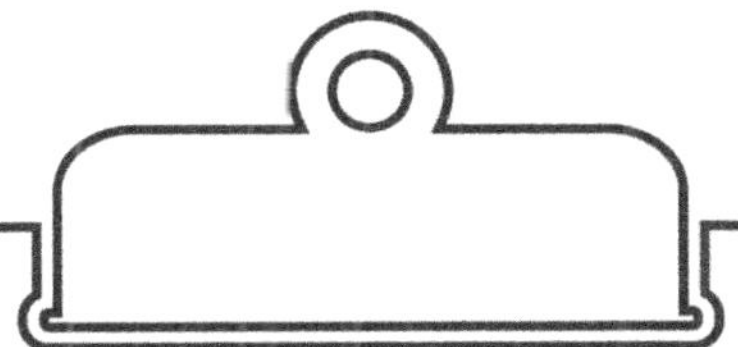

Requirement One: Follow up

DO THIS TODAY

- ☐ Schedule a 15-minute A-B-C Check-in with each of your direct reports this week.
- ☐ Pick one team and organize its responsibilities into A, B, and C categories.
- ☐ Create a checklist for what you want to hear in each check-in (focus on B and C).
- ☐ Set a calendar reminder for a monthly performance evaluation conversation.
- ☐ Ask one team member, "Where do you need more input? And where can I step back?"

REQUIREMENT TWO:

RESOLVE DESTRUCTIVE CONFLICT

Conflict in the workplace can be good. In fact, it can be a necessary thing for your organization's success. But only—only—if it's constructive conflict. Constructive conflict occurs in the space where ideas come together and collide in a search for the best path to success. It is the purifying process that occurs when a team searches for the truth or works to forge the strategy that will give it the best opportunity for success.

If ideas never collide constructively in your team, you are probably far too authoritarian in your management style and in your delegation style. If people never speak up about their work and tell you things that you might not want to hear, they are probably scared, not empowered. True ownership will push your people to speak up respectfully to you and to their peers as they push for what they believe in.

But there is conflict that is not constructive. In fact, there is conflict that is purely destructive. It is the conflict that becomes personal, the conflict that generates confusion, and the conflict that obscures a clear mission.

Few things will derail your **A-B-C Delegation** (or any delegation system, for that matter) faster than unresolved, destructive conflict. When conflict is small, it may feel easy to ignore, but left alone, it spreads. It can leap from person to person, and from one department to another, infecting culture and undermining the mission. Your job as a manager is to detect and resolve conflict early. Always.

Resolving Destructive Conflict has Three Fundamental Components:

2.1 – IDENTIFY & RESOLVE

The three types of destructive conflict: Personal, Mission, and Systemic Conflict.

2.2 – REMOVE IT

If resolution fails, remove the source of conflict for the sake of the team and for the sake of the mission.

2.3 – STAY PROFESSIONAL

Confront the issue head-on, but keep your cool: Be courageous, direct, and honest. But stay professional.

RESOLVE DESTRUCTIVE CONFLICT – 2.1

Identify & Resolve

If constructive conflict arises, this can be good for your team if you manage it well. But, as a manager, you'll see three recurring types of destructive conflict. Each affects your **A-B-C Delegation** system differently...but all will undermine it if left unresolved.

The three types of destructive conflict are:

PERSONAL CONFLICT

MISSION CONFLICT

SYSTEMIC CONFLICT

Each of these types of conflict gets worse with time. They drain energy, productivity, and trust. If employees don't trust the people or processes around them, they'll stop owning their responsibilities or start bypassing you altogether.

Your job as a manager is to name the conflict, act early, and restore alignment before the damage spreads. Be bold, be courageous, and tackle every destructive conflict that you detect head-on.

Identify & Resolve

The First Type of Destructive Conflict: Personal Conflict

This is the most common type of destructive conflict that you will encounter: interpersonal friction rooted in personality, communication styles, or simply a lack of mutual respect. Sometimes it's the tone of an email. Sometimes, two people just don't like each other.

Personal Conflict is not about the mission. It's a distraction from the work that occurs when two or more people focus on each other instead of on the goal.

Don't let it fester. Personal Conflict spreads fast and can become a toxin in your team culture. It will do tremendous damage to your **A-B-C Delegation**, so address it directly and early.

If you want your team to operate with purpose and direction, everyone must have the space to fully contribute, regardless of background or personality. The standard must be clear: leave personal differences at the door.

To resolve Personal Conflict, sit down with the individuals involved. Put the problem on the table—figuratively—and ask them to address it without pointing fingers or referencing each other personally. If they can't separate the issue from their emotions about the person in front of them, then it's probably not a work-related problem, but a personal one, and it doesn't belong at work.

You don't need your team to be best friends. You need them to collaborate professionally and stay aligned with the mission and values of the organization. Purely personal issues must not be allowed to disrupt that.

HOW TO SAY IT:

Resolving Personal Conflict

Starter Lines: Use these to set the frame and shift focus to the work:

- "We're not here to discuss personalities. We're here to protect the mission."
- "I expect professionalism, even when personal dynamics are tough."
- "Let's bring this back to outcomes and responsibilities."

1. Mentoring Approach

Supportive, values-driven tone

- "I know conflict is uncomfortable, but we can work through it with professionalism and shared purpose."
- "You both care about the work. Let's find a way to focus that energy constructively."
- "You don't need to be friends, but you do need to be respectful collaborators."

2. Firm Approach

Clear expectations and redirection

- "This is no longer about a disagreement. It's becoming a distraction from the mission. That must stop."
- "We're here to deliver results, not to referee personal dynamics. Leave that at the door."
- "You are both responsible for maintaining a professional environment. That's part of your job."

3. Tough Approach

No-nonsense, non-negotiable stance

- "This behavior is damaging the team. It ends now. If it doesn't, there will be consequences."
- "I don't care if you like each other. I care that the work gets done without drama."
- "You're both accountable for professionalism. If you can't meet that standard, we'll reevaluate your fit on this team."

Closing Lines: Use these to re-anchor the conversation on progress and professionalism:

- "We're moving forward from this. I expect both of you to raise concerns professionally and stay mission-focused."
- "You have a responsibility to each other and

to the team. Let's see that reflected in your actions."

- "This is your opportunity to rebuild trust. Take it seriously."

Takeaway: When resolving personal conflict, strip it of emotion and redirect focus to professionalism. Use mentoring to de-escalate, firmness to realign, and toughness to enforce standards when necessary.

Example:

Resolving Personal Conflict

Characters:

- Riley (Marketing Director)
- Jordan (Project Manager)
- Zara (COO)

Background:

Riley and Jordan are strong performers, but their working relationship has deteriorated. Riley finds Jordan slow to act and overly cautious. Jordan finds Riley abrasive and dismissive of team input. Their emails have gotten tense. Meetings are stiff. Other team members sense the rift and try to keep them apart. What started as a difference in style is beginning to feel personal.

The Manager's Move:

Zara, their COO, steps in, not to force agreement, but to get the focus back where it belongs: the work.

Zara: "Thanks for sitting down with me. I've been observing the dynamic between you two, and I need to name it: it's affecting the team. I know this isn't about who's a good person or who's right. But it is about the work."

Jordan: "I've honestly been avoiding projects with Riley. It feels like there's no point in speaking up. My input gets waved off."

Riley: "And I've been frustrated because projects get stalled waiting for every angle to be reviewed. It slows us down."

Zara: "That's real. And I'm not here to smooth that over. But here's what I want to put on the table."

She pulls out the quarterly objectives.

Zara: "These are the campaigns and deliverables we're accountable for in Q3. This isn't about your preferences, it's about what the mission needs. We need fast execution and thoughtful risk management. Neither of you can deliver that alone."

Together, they begin working through:

- Which types of decisions Riley can make without Jordan's input.
- Where Jordan's oversight is critical and needs to be honored.
- A clear rule: critique the work, not the person.

Zara: "I don't need you to like each other more. I need you to focus your energy on this work. And I'm going to check back in two weeks to see how it's going."

Why It Worked:

- Zara didn't avoid the conflict. Instead, she named it.
- Instead of making it personal, she made it mission-driven.
- She re-centered the conversation on shared deliverables, not personality traits.

Takeaway:

When the conflict is personal, shift the focus to the work. Don't ask people to change who they are. Instead, ask them to change how they collaborate.

Identify & Resolve

The Second Type of Destructive Conflict: Mission Conflict

Mission Conflict occurs when:

- There's no shared understanding of the organization's goals.
- An individual is misaligned with the mission.
- Someone acts against the organization's values.

Sometimes the impact is quiet at first. A single dissenting team member might seem manageable until others start following their lead. If unaddressed, motivation, alignment, and morale will begin to erode across the team. Left to fester, your team will lose faith in you and in the responsibility that you want them to take ownership of.

Mission Conflict may be a disagreement over what the mission actually means, or a clash in how to pursue it. Correct misalignment immediately because a team cannot move forward at maximum efficiency if even one person is pulling in the wrong direction.

The solution? Bring the team back to the mission and values. Anchor the conversation there.

If the conflict stems from differing interpretations of direction, bring the parties together and lay out their opposing views. Look at your organization's **Mission Frame**, and if one interpretation is clearly aligned with it, say so. If not, make a call and clarify it.

If it's a judgment call, make the judgment. Defining the direction of the team is one of your most important responsibilities as a leader.

Once a decision is made, make it clear that you expect unity moving forward. If someone disagrees with the chosen path, the standard must be Bezos' famous line from his 2016 shareholder letter: "disagree and commit."

Mission Conflict left unresolved erodes alignment and weakens momentum. Your team won't aim in the same direction if they aren't clear on what they're aiming for.

HOW TO SAY IT:

Resolving Mission Conflict

Starter Lines: Open the discussion with focus on clarity and shared direction:

- "Let's revisit the mission and align our decisions accordingly."
- "If we're pulling in different directions, we need to fix that right now."
- "I want to hear your perspectives, then clarify what the mission requires from us."

1. Mentoring Approach

Collaborative, alignment-building tone

- "I see where you're coming from, and I value the passion behind it. Let's align that energy to our shared mission."
- "It's okay to disagree. What matters is that we commit to the same direction afterward."
- "Your point of view is valid, but we need to operate as one team moving toward one goal."

2. Firm Approach

Clear decision-making and redirection

- "The mission must guide our actions. From this point forward, this is the direction we're taking."

- "You may have a different interpretation, but this decision is final. I need your full commitment."
- "This isn't about who's right. It's about aligning to what the organization needs."

3. Tough Approach

Decisive, authority-driven tone

- "This is not optional. If you can't align with the mission and direction, we need to reevaluate your role here."
- "We're not debating the mission anymore. We're executing on it."
- "This continued resistance is an unnecessary distraction. That won't be tolerated."

Closing Lines: End by reaffirming shared commitment:

- "I expect unity moving forward."
- "Now that the direction is clear, your role is to help lead others into alignment."
- "This team thrives when we aim in the same direction. Let's get there together."

Takeaway: Mission conflict is about misalignment, not always malice. Use mentoring to build buy-in, firmness to clarify direction, and toughness when unity must override individual preferences.

Example:

Resolving Mission Conflict

Characters:

- Amira (Product Manager)
- Leo (Software Engineer)

The Conflict:

The company's mission is: "To empower people through intuitive, cutting-edge digital tools." Amira prioritizes user experience; Leo prioritizes advanced features. They clash over a confusing feature Amira wants removed. Leo accuses her of "dumbing down" the product, amd meetings become tense. Leo starts making unilateral changes. Amira vents to other teams, and trust begins to erode.

Manager's Intervention:

The manager refocuses them on the mission: innovation and usability. They agree to test both versions with users and let data guide the decision.

Why It Worked:

- The manager anchors the discussion in the mission.
- Both perspectives are respected and aligned.
- Clarity replaces conflict.

Takeaway:

When team members interpret the mission differently, leadership must clarify direction. Mission conflict isn't personal, but if left unresolved, it can be. Resolve it early by aligning everyone to the purpose.

Identify & Resolve

The Third Type of Destructive Conflict: Systemic Conflict

Systemic Conflict arises from unclear processes or responsibilities. It's structural, not personal. One department may inadvertently create more work for another. Team members may be duplicating efforts or missing critical handoffs because expectations were never clearly defined.

Left unresolved, this kind of friction:

- Slows everything down.
- Wastes time and energy.
- Signals to your team that leadership doesn't care.

Clarity is the cure. You may not need to redesign the whole system, but you must name the friction and fix it.

System Conflict is often one of the simplest for a manager to fix, and it is dangerous to ignore.

Start by reviewing the process. Identify the source of friction, and if internal workflows are vague, overlapping, or inefficient, revise them.

If the friction comes from external requirements like regulations, compliance standards, or government mandates, acknowledge the frustration but reinforce reality: *some things are just part of the terrain.* A delivery company can't change the height of the mountain. It just has to find the best route over it.

But when the friction is internal, it's your job to smooth the path. Discomfort with a process can quickly turn into personal resentment if left unresolved.

A broken system, if ignored, becomes a breeding ground for inefficiency and for Personal Conflict.

HOW TO SAY IT:

Resolving Systemic Conflict

Starter Lines: Start the conversation by identifying structural issues:

- "Let's talk about where the process is breaking down."
- "This looks like a system issue, not a people issue."
- "We need to clarify roles and workflows to avoid future friction."

1. Mentoring Approach

Supportive, problem-solving tone

- "I know this isn't about effort. It's about structure. Let's fix the system together."
- "If we improve the process, we improve performance. And your work will get easier, too."
- "What changes would make your role clearer and more efficient?"

2. Firm Approach

Clarity- and alignment-focused tone

- "Here's how we're going to move forward: [define process]. I expect you to follow it."

- "We're aligning workflows now to reduce confusion. Even if it's not your preferred method, I need your commitment."
- "This adjustment supports the entire team. Your role in that matters."

3. Tough Approach

Decisive, accountability-centered tone

- "This process is no longer up for debate. We're doing it this way to prevent future breakdowns."
- "If you continue working around the system, you're undermining the team. That won't continue."
- "Resistance to a clear process isn't just frustrating. It's damaging. I need full alignment."

Closing Lines: Reinforce the plan and expectations:

- "I'll be checking in to see how the new structure is working...and that it's being followed."
- "Thank you for engaging constructively. Let's make this smoother for everyone."
- "With this clarity in place, I expect smoother collaboration and fewer escalations."

Takeaway: Systemic conflict stems from unclear structure. Use mentoring to co-create solutions, firmness to enforce clarity, and toughness to shut down resistance to necessary change.

Example:

Resolving Systemic Conflict

Characters:

- Elena (Customer Experience Director)
- Priya (Product Manager)
- Andre (Support Team Lead)

Background:

Customer satisfaction scores have dropped sharply. The Support team says product bugs are to blame. The Product team says Support keeps reporting issues without clear data or reproduction steps. Each team thinks the other is failing to do their job. A subtle blame cycle has formed, but no one's openly hostile yet.

The Conflict:

Elena begins hearing frustration from both sides in weekly meetings. Everyone seems defensive, projects are stalling, and customers are waiting too long for real fixes. Elena suspects it's not about attitudes but about broken handoffs and vague expectations.

She calls a joint working session.

Elena: "Thanks for making time. I want to be very clear: I don't believe this is about people not caring. I believe we have a system problem and that system is breaking the trust between your teams."

Andre: "We log every issue with the product team, but they don't act on most of them. We're doing our job."

Priya: "And we'd love to fix them, but we get vague bug reports with no reproduction steps. If we can't recreate it, we can't fix it. We're not ignoring anything."

Elena: "This is exactly what I mean. Both of you are right from your side. But from the customer's side, we're failing. Let's map the process step by step and find where the breakdowns happen."

Elena draws a timeline on the whiteboard. Together, they uncover several issues:

- Support uses language in tickets that isn't aligned with Product's terminology.
- Product doesn't see the full ticket history, just summarized reports.
- Some tools don't sync between systems, so updates are missed or duplicated.

Elena: "Here's the good news: this is all solvable. We don't have a people problem, we have a system without lanes. Let's fix that."

She proposes:

1. A shared ticket template for escalations that includes specific reproduction steps.
2. A weekly 30-minute triage meeting between Support and Product reps.
3. A glossary of terms and tagging system both teams agree to use.

Priya: "I can live with that. If we get cleaner reports, we can respond faster."

Andre: "And if we get feedback loops on what happens to tickets, we'll know we're not just sending things into the void."

Elena: "Great. I'll help launch this process and check back in a month. But it's on both of you to own it after that."

Why It Worked:

- Elena reframed the problem from "you vs. them" to "us vs. the process."
- She didn't let silence or indirect tension linger.
- She created structural fixes that both sides contributed to and felt ownership over.

RESOLVE DESTRUCTIVE CONFLICT – 2.2
Remove It

If an employee is consistently underperforming despite clear interventions, you need to act. Doing nothing sends a dangerous message to your team: that excellence doesn't matter, and that destructive conflict and indifference are acceptable. High performers will lose motivation if they see low standards being tolerated, and the responsibility that each employee will feel for their **Mandate Frame** will erode.

If someone has been given every reasonable opportunity to improve and still can't meet expectations, it's time for them to leave the team. Don't consider this cruelty. What's cruel is keeping someone in a role they're not suited for and expecting the rest of your team to carry the burden.

If you've done the work to coach, clarify, and redirect them, and they still resist change, it may be time for them to go find an organization that's a better fit.

A-B-C Delegation works best when your team is aligned. If someone is consistently generating conflict or falling short despite your best efforts, they cannot be allowed to drag down the mission. The livelihood of each individual matters, but not at the cost of the health and momentum of the entire team.

HOW TO DO IT:

The "One-Dealbreaker Conversation"

If you've made a sincere effort to bring someone back into alignment and they still refuse to engage productively, take these steps:

- Identify the issue: Is it Personal Conflict, Mission Conflict, or Systemic Conflict? Or is the problem one of capacity or attitude?
- Attempt resolution: Coach, redirect, train, retrain, and set clear expectations.
- Document everything: Protect your integrity and your organization from legal risk.
- Then, if necessary, let them go in a professional manner.

If you must fire someone, use the "ONE-DEALBREAKER CONVERSATION" to avoid unnecessary complications.

- Don't list every frustration you've ever had with them. That invites debate.
- Focus on a single, undeniable violation that crosses a clear boundary. If you give them ten reasons to argue with, they will often pick the weakest and derail the conversation.
- Be firm, respectful, and consistent. Firing should not be emotional. It should be a clear outcome based on behavior that cannot continue.

RESOLVE DESTRUCTIVE CONFLICT – 2.3
Stay Professional

This should be obvious to any manager. It should be obvious to any serious professional. But for **A-B-C Delegation** to work, professional behavior and maintaining calm in the storm are crucial. If you let yourself lose it and succumb to your emotions, your leadership will not get stronger, but weaker. Your team will not grow stronger, but weaker.

When implementing these practical fixes for destructive conflict in your **A-B-C Delegation** system, consider two general rules that will save you time, effort, and nerves in the long run:

- Shuffling problems only creates new problems; and
- Anger is not a management tool.

Don't Shuffle Problems

Moving a burning issue from one area to another doesn't extinguish it. It just spreads the fire.

Too often, managers try to sidestep tough conversations by relocating the problem, reassigning a difficult employee, shifting a personality conflict across departments, or creating lateral moves to buy time. But unless you truly believe a person's skills are better suited elsewhere, moving them won't solve the issue.

If someone refuses to align with the mission in one role, they likely won't do it in another. If they reject structure or systems in one place, they'll do the same in their next team. And if they carry Personal Conflict that they're unwilling to resolve, they'll likely recreate it somewhere new.

Resolve conflict before any moves, and let relocation be a reward for growth, not an escape hatch from accountability. If an employee requests a transfer due to a conflict, ask them to demonstrate their ability to engage professionally first, because if they can't, you don't want them elsewhere.

Anger Is Not a Management Tool

Anger isn't leadership or strength. It's a loss of control.

Some managers think anger shows passion or commitment. It doesn't. It creates fear, not respect. Worse, it distracts from the issue, erodes trust, and silences initiative.

A-B-C Delegation thrives in a culture of ownership, not fear. When people worry more about your reaction than the results, they stop taking initiative. They wait for orders, and innovation dies.

Yes, leadership involves emotion, but your job is to stay composed. A calm, firm response with clear expectations and follow-through is far more effective than yelling.

Anger kills courage, and it shifts focus from the mission to survival. Over time, your team will stop trying, choosing safety over growth.

Great leaders don't lash out. They lead with clarity, consistency, and control, so set the tone, stay steady, and lead with respect.

Summary: Resolving Destructive Conflict

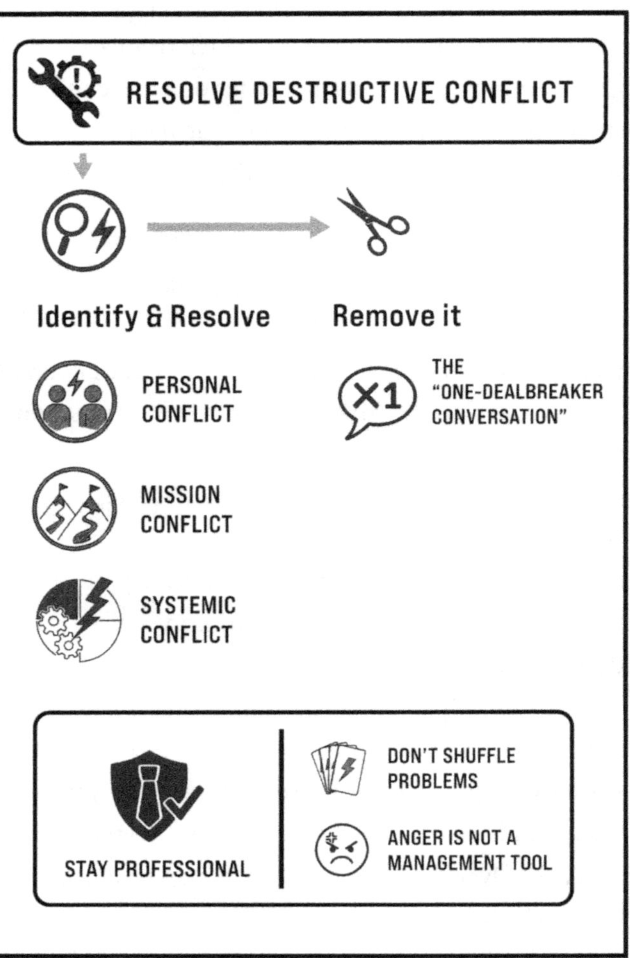

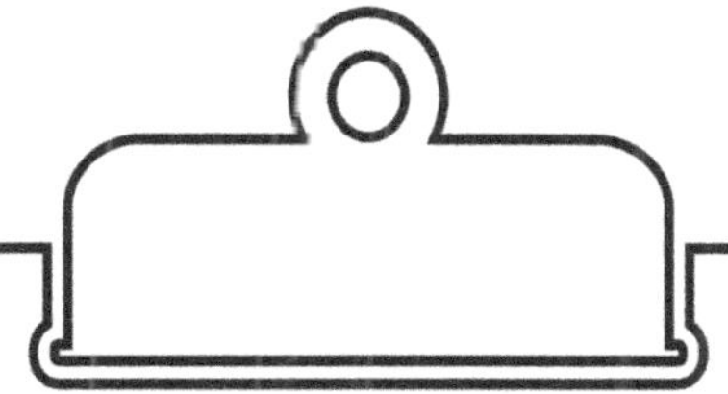

Requirement Two: Resolve Destructive Conflict

DO THIS TODAY

- ☐ Identify one conflict in your team and decide: Personal, Mission, or Systemic?
- ☐ Draft a script for how you'll address that conflict using a mentoring, firm, or tough tone.
- ☐ Commit to confronting, not avoiding, one problem you've let slide.
- ☐ Choose one team standard (e.g., professionalism, communication) and reinforce it in your next team meeting.
- ☐ Reflect: Have you been shuffling problems or letting anger lead? Adjust accordingly.

REQUIREMENT THREE:

DEVELOP NEW LEADERS

A-B-C Delegation isn't just a system for managing work. It's a tool for building leadership that knows how to manage work. Used well, it becomes a self-reinforcing cycle, a virtuous loop of clarity, responsibility, and growth. It allows managers to delegate with structure while identifying and developing the next generation of leaders inside the organization.

To build a proactive, high-performing team, not just task-completers, you must do three things:

3.1 BUILD CAPACITY

Train your people. Prepare them for the work that you expect of them.

3.2 CREATE OPPORTUNITY

Offer meaningful paths to growth for everyone.

3.3 CULTIVATE RESPONSIBILITY

Build a culture of ownership and initiative.

DEVELOP NEW LEADERS – 3.1 Build Capacity

Elk and gazelles are born ready to run. Some sharks can detect predators while still in the egg. But most professionals? They need training.

You cannot delegate effectively to someone who doesn't know how to do the job, and expecting great results without preparation is not delegation. It's setting them up to fail.

If you want your team to deliver, you must train them first. But don't stop at current responsibilities. If you want to build future leaders, your training must be forward-looking. Equip your team not only for today's work but also for the roles they'll grow into tomorrow.

Think of capacity as a muscle: it strengthens with deliberate effort and support. Here's how to build it:

Onboarding

New team members don't just need instructions, they need orientation. Onboarding should provide context, expectations, and clarity on where they fit in the mission and within their Mandate Frame.

Set the tone early and make it clear that ownership is the goal, not just task completion. If they understand **A-B-C Delegation** from day one, they'll step into responsibility faster and with more confidence.

On-the-Job Training

Learning doesn't end after onboarding. Ongoing training is how you move people from reliance to resilience. Whether it's shadowing, structured feedback, or stretch assignments, build learning into the workflow, not around it.

The best training is intentional, embedded in real work, and tied directly to the Mandate Frame. Don't isolate it into side projects or generic sessions, and instead, teach in the flow of work, and evaluate as they go.

Develop the Judgment to Match the Skill

Technical skill is important, but judgment is what makes **A-B-C Delegation** work. A team member might be great at executing tasks, but if they don't know when to escalate or when to inform you, the system breaks down.

Use regular check-ins to build this judgment. Debrief after decisions. Ask questions like:

"How did you decide this was a Category B, not C?"

"What would you do differently next time?"

"What context do you need to make better calls?"

Over time, they'll internalize the framework. And when they start classifying tasks accurately without asking you every time, you'll know they're ready for more.

Train for What's Next, Not Just What's Now

Don't just train people for the jobs they have. Train them for the jobs they want, and the roles they might step into.

If you wait until someone is promoted to start preparing them, you've waited too long.

Proactive capacity-building looks like:

- Giving someone lead responsibility on a cross-functional project.
- Letting them handle a Category C decision under your supervision.
- Inviting them to shadow you in strategic meetings.

Each of these moments says: *I see your potential—and I'm investing in it.*

Takeaway

You can't scale your leadership if your team doesn't grow with you, so training isn't optional. It's how you protect the mission, empower your people, and build a team capable of leading without your constant involvement.

Before you delegate, ask yourself if the person has the skill to take on the responsibility that you want to give them. And ask yourself if they have the judgment to handle the responsibility that you want to give them.

Make a plan to invest in their capacity and in their

judgment, because once they're ready, the real delegation can begin.

HOW TO SAY IT:
Building Capacity

Starter Lines:

Set the tone that growth is the goal:

- "I want to help you to build your ability to lead more, not just do more."
- "You've got a strong foundation. Let's develop the skills and judgment for what comes next."
- "This isn't about dumping tasks, it's about preparing you to own more."

1. Mentoring Approach

Supportive, growth-focused

- "Let's structure a few shadowing opportunities so you can see how I approach this."
- "You're not expected to have it all figured out. That's what training is for."
- "I'll coach you on the why, not just the how, so you grow in confidence and clarity."

2. Firm Approach

Performance-driven, expectation-setting

- "Before I can delegate more, I need to see consistency and clear judgment."
- "I'll walk you through the first round. After

that, I expect you to try leading it yourself."
- "You're capable. To grow here, I need you to learn this."

3. Tough Approach

High-accountability, growth-challenging

- "If you want more responsibility, you need to build the skill and judgment to match it."
- "This is your stretch zone. Step up now."
- "Growth doesn't happen by waiting. It happens by doing hard things, prepared and supported."

Closing Lines:

Wrap with clear commitment and support:

- "This is your training ground. Let's make it count."
- "Prove you're ready. I'm here to back you, but you need to lead the effort."
- "When you master this, the next level is yours."

Example:

Building Capacity

Characters:

- Sofia (Director of Development)
- David (New Grants Manager)

Background: David joined recently with strong writing skills but limited organizational experience. His Mandate Frame includes donor communications and smaller grant proposals (Category A), but he's eager to take on large-scale proposals and partnerships (currently Category C). Sofia sees potential but knows David needs coaching and context before advancing his scope.

The Conversation:

Sofia: "David, you've been doing a great job managing donor updates and handling our smaller grants. I want to talk about your growth path."

David: "I appreciate that. I'd really like to work on our bigger proposals too. I feel ready to contribute more."

Sofia: "I like your initiative. Here's how we'll build toward that. I want you to shadow me through the next two proposals. I'll loop you into planning meetings and give you drafts to review, and then I'll ask you to write one section solo, and we'll review it together."

David: "Sounds great. I learn best by doing."

Sofia: "Exactly. And as we go, I'll talk through which tasks are Category B and which are Category C, and why. You'll build the judgment, not just the skills."

David: "That's helpful. I've been unsure where the lines are, and I want to get that right."

Sofia: "You will. You've shown the right mindset. And once you're ready, I'll move parts of this into your Mandate Frame."

Why It Worked:

- Clear training plan with increasing responsibility.
- Real-time judgment coaching within the A-B-C framework.
- Encouragement without over-promotion.

DEVELOP NEW LEADERS – 3.2
Create Opportunity

A-B-C Delegation thrives on untapping the potential of every team member. For it to succeed, it must be adopted across the whole organization, because any part of the team that suppresses growth becomes a drag on everyone else's momentum.

Start with your direct reports. Give them a chance to shine, but also expect them to do the same for their teams. The goal is to create an environment where everyone sees a path to grow.

But opportunity without alignment can lead your organization off-track. That's why the best leaders take time to understand their employees' goals, not just for the team, but personally and professionally.

Opportunity Through Alignment

Consider your goals and the goals of your team. Just like you, every employee has three types of goals:

- **Organizational goals:** within your company or organization.
- **Professional goals:** their long-term career ambitions (maybe in your organization, maybe elsewhere).

- **Personal goals:** what matters to them outside of work.

If you are the CEO of the company, your goals may look like this:

- **Organizational goals:** the Mission Frame of the organization.
- **Professional goals:** job growth, greater responsibility, either within the organization or later in a larger company. Maybe an industry change?
- **Personal goals:** family goals (children, etc.) and hobbies (skydiving, crochet, etc.).

And one of your employees may have goals that look like this:

- **Organizational goals:** their Mandate Frame in your organization, plus additional areas of interest for future responsibility.
- **Professional goals:** job growth, either within or outside of the organization.
- **Personal goals:** family goals (holiday home in Aspen) and hobbies (skiing, hiking, etc.).

It will help you to find alignment between your employees' goals, your own goals, and your organization's goals.

See the Diagram: Alignment of Goals

Have a look at the illustration below. Your employees' goals have four parts, three of which overlap with yours:

[1] Their Mandate Frame (what they already own).

[2] Other goals they have within the organization (e.g., promotion, new responsibilities).

[3] Personal or professional interests outside the organization that overlap with yours.

[4] Goals outside your awareness, unrelated to you.

You shouldn't pry into your team's personal ambitions. But the more they choose to share their goals, the more you can help and the more they'll want to help you reach your goals, too.

Understand your overlaps with the goals of your employees, and you will be able to support them to achieve the success that they want. If you can do this and commit yourself to helping them, they will see you not only as a boss, but as an ally for the success that they desire.

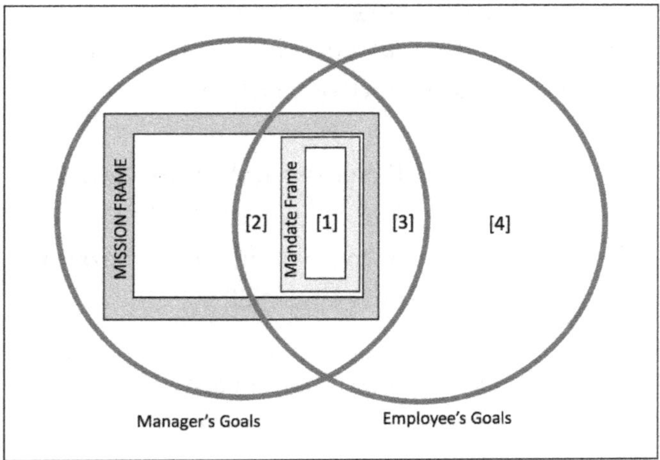

Consider how you can help committed employees to achieve their goals. Ask yourself:

- Can you help them grow in their current responsibilities? Can you expand their Mandate Frame (area [1])? Can you move activities from Category C to Category B, or Category B to Category A?
- Can you give them new responsibilities in the workplace (see area [2])?
- Consider if you can help them grow in a way that will benefit their professional goals, even if they lie outside of your organization (see area [3]). Maybe through training that they need, or connections that you have with other companies?
- Are there accommodations that you can make in the workplace so that the employee can

> better balance their other goals (see area [4])? Maybe personal goals, including those that don't overlap with yours? Maybe time to attend an important family event, or a course that they will need for a new job that they are preparing for elsewhere?

People are more likely to give their best if they know that their best will help them achieve their dreams, and that their manager is there to support them in their dreams.

HOW TO SAY IT:

Creating Opportunity

Starter Lines: Set a positive and growth-oriented tone:

- "You've been doing excellent work, and I want to talk about your growth path."
- "Let's look at how we can expand your impact and support your goals."
- "You've shown strong ownership. Let's build on that."

1. Mentoring Approach

Supportive, long-term investment tone

- "I want to support you in reaching your professional and personal goals, whether that's here or beyond."
- "You've proven yourself in your current scope. What areas would you like to grow into next?"
- "This is a place to grow. I want you to succeed here and in your larger goals."

2. Firm Approach

Direct, performance-driven tone

- "You've demonstrated capability at this level. I'm officially expanding your responsibility starting now."
- "You're ready for the next step. I'll move

this task from Category C to B, and I expect continued strong judgment."

- "This isn't just more work. It's an opportunity to lead at a higher level, so treat it that way."

3. Tough Approach
Challenge-oriented, urgency-driven tone

- "If you want to grow, you need to step up. I'm giving you this opportunity, but I want to see you prove that you can own it."
- "Leadership means acting without waiting to be told. This is your chance to show you're ready."
- "Staying comfortable isn't growth. I'm expecting you to stretch now, not later."

Closing Lines: End with encouragement and next steps:

- "You've earned this opportunity. Now, let's keep building."
- "I'll support you, but this is your next level. Let's see it."
- "Keep the communication strong, and keep showing initiative. That's what growth looks like."

Takeaway: Creating opportunity is about recognizing readiness and supporting ambition. Use mentoring to align with goals, firmness to formalize advancement, and toughness to drive growth when it's overdue.

Example:

Creating Opportunity

Characters:

- Tasha (Director of Strategic Initiatives)
- Samira (Senior Associate)

Background: Samira quickly embraced A-B-C Delegation:

- **Category A:** Routine partner check-ins, meeting logistics
- **Category B:** Drafting pilot plans, stakeholder updates
- **Category C:** Final pilot approvals, major budget discussions

She delivered consistently, flagged Category C items early, and demonstrated strong judgment and initiative.

The Conversation:

Tasha: "Samira, I want to talk with you today not because something's wrong, but because so much is going right. You've been managing your Mandate Frame with clarity and confidence. The way you approach Category C items, not just with questions, but with solid recommendations, shows you're already thinking like a senior leader."

Samira: "Thanks, Tasha. I've really tried to internalize the A-B-C model and think ahead. It helps me know where I stand and what's expected."

Tasha: "It shows. That's why I'm expanding your responsibilities. From now on, you can handle early-stage partner negotiations and draft preliminary budgets without needing prior approval. Just keep me informed. Those move from Category C to B."

Samira: "Wow. I've been hoping for something like this. I want to keep growing and contribute more strategically."

Tasha: "You're ready. If this goes well, I'll likely move some Category B tasks into A next quarter, like operational approvals you've already mastered. This isn't just more work. It's the next step in your growth here."

Samira: "That means a lot. What would you like from me as I take this on?"

Tasha: "Keep doing what you're doing: proactive updates, good judgment, and clear communication. And if you hit a snag, I'm here. Let's keep building from here."

Why It Worked:

- Recognition is specific and performance-based.
- New responsibility is clearly defined and empowering.
- The conversation reinforces trust, growth, and structure.

Takeaway:

Delegation isn't just about offloading tasks, it's about recognizing potential and creating opportunities. Done right, it builds leaders from within.

Opportunity for everyone

If a manager gives responsibility to their direct reports but they, in turn, do not give any responsibility to their respective teams, the organization cannot work at its best.

While organizational culture is determined top-down, work flows bottom-up, and if you have bottlenecks, efficiency will suffer. Then you as the manager will not be receiving the whole volume of work from your team that you could be receiving.

For effective **A-B-C Delegation**, everyone must be given the chance to work at their maximum efficiency, effectiveness, and authority. To remove obstacles to efficiency, ensure that every middle-manager is implementing **A-B-C Delegation** with their team. Each person in the hierarchical chain of the organization can slow the progress of the whole if they are not working at full capacity, authority, and efficiency.

HOW TO SAY IT:

Opportunity for Everyone

Starter Lines: Frame the conversation around scaling delegation and leadership:

- "You've mastered A-B-C Delegation with me. Now it's time to extend that clarity to your team."
- "Strong leadership isn't just about how you communicate up. It's about how you build leaders below you."
- "Let's talk about how you can multiply your impact by empowering your team."

1. Mentoring Approach

Supportive, growth-focused tone

- "You've shown great judgment. Now let's focus on building that same judgment in your team."
- "Think of your next step not as doing more, but enabling others to do more."
- "Let's map out how your team can take on more ownership like you have."

2. Firm Approach

Clear, leadership-standard tone

- "If your team can't move without you, delegation is breaking down. It's your job to fix that."
- "You've been delegated responsibility. Now you need to delegate it to your team."
- "Every level of leadership must implement A-B-C Delegation. I expect you to do that starting now."

3. Tough Approach

Challenging, accountability-focused tone

- "True leadership is proven by how you develop those below you."
- "If you're the only one owning, you're hoarding responsibility, not leading. That has to change."
- "You're not here to control everything. You're here to build people who can deliver without your constant involvement."

Closing Lines: End by reinforcing expectations and leadership scope:

- "You have the tools. Now use them to build clarity and ownership within your team."
- "This isn't optional. Effective delegation must scale through every level of this organization."

- "You've earned trust. Now share it and grow your team the same way."

Takeaway: Opportunity must cascade. Use mentoring to inspire growth, firmness to set leadership expectations, and toughness to break bottlenecks and scale responsibility.

Example:

Creating Opportunity (for Everyone!)

Characters:

- Leila (Director of Programs)
- Noah (Psychology Department Lead)

Background: Noah embraced A-B-C Delegation with his boss, Leila:

- **Category A:** Session scheduling, daily reporting
- **Category B:** Program design, partnership proposals
- **Category C:** Budget approvals, staffing changes

But within his own team, Noah micromanaged. He gave vague assignments, double-checked basic work, and became the bottleneck. Talented staff hesitated to act, and efficiency dropped.

The Conversation:

Leila: "Noah, you've been a strong A-B-C Delegator with me. I always know what you own, and you bring me the right Category C decisions. But I'm noticing a gap in how that structure flows to your team."

Noah: "Really? I've been trying to stay close to the work to avoid mistakes."

Leila: "I understand that instinct. But holding on too tightly limits your team's growth, and yours as well. Your success isn't just about what you deliver; it's about how you lead. Your team needs their own Mandate Frames, and they need to know what they can handle without you."

Noah: "Honestly, I wasn't sure they were ready."

Leila: "Then help them get there. Build their judgment the way I built yours. A-B-C Delegation isn't just upward. It must cascade, otherwise, you become a bottleneck."

Noah: "Got it. I'll start by defining their Mandate Frames and clarifying categories."

Leila: "Good. And hold regular check-ins the way we do. The more you invest in their autonomy, the more time and trust you'll gain. Leadership at scale means empowering others to lead."

Why It Worked:

- Leila connected Noah's strengths to a leadership gap.
- She framed growth as a next-level skill, not a critique.
- Delegation was expanded from a personal habit to a team standard.

Takeaway:

Effective delegation must scale. If middle managers don't replicate the model, the whole system slows. Empowerment can't stop at the top.

DEVELOP NEW LEADERS – 3.3
Cultivate Responsibility

True delegation flourishes when everyone on the team feels true responsibility for their work. It happens when everyone not only carries out their tasks responsibly, but when they feel a commitment to foster and grow everything that is in their Mandate Frame. Responsibility turns passive task-doers into proactive leaders who embrace their role, anticipate challenges, and take initiative.

By modeling values, encouraging accountability, and creating a culture where mistakes are seen as learning opportunities, you deepen the trust and responsibility that make **A-B-C Delegation** effective. This chapter is about helping your team step into leadership. Not someday, but today.

Model the Values

Show your team what you expect through both words and actions. Start with a clear mission and vision, but don't stop there. Define your organizational values in writing, communicate them consistently, and, most importantly, live them yourself.

When behavior aligns with those values, recognize it. When it doesn't, address it. Ignoring misalignment weakens responsibility, invites conflict, and erodes team cohesion.

There are two essentials to modeling values:

- Clearly define and communicate your organization's values.
- Embody those values in your daily behavior and decisions.

If you demand what you don't demonstrate, your credibility suffers. People won't give their best to a leader they perceive as hypocritical. But when your team sees you uphold the values you promote, they'll hold themselves, and each other, to that same standard.

In short: be the best example of what you want to see.

Ownership Leads to Responsibility

To cultivate responsibility, reinforce with each person who works for you that you trust them with their Mandate Frame, their personal piece of the organization's mission. Tell them it's not blind trust and that you'll still check in, support, and evaluate, but that you've made a conscious decision to delegate real ownership and to trust them with a piece of what is everyone's. Don't let your team get passive, only working on a task "because the boss said so." The more of a sense of ownership that you inspire, the more responsibility your team will feel for their Mandate Frame, and the more your team will give you their best work every day.

Talk to your team about this openly. Conversations

on ownership shift the mindset from task-doers to mission-owners. They help employees see their role not just a job, but a domain they are responsible for improving.

Ownership deepens when people are asked to reflect on it.

Learn from Mistakes

Your team's relationship with failure matters. If mistakes are treated only as punishable offenses, you will create a culture of fear and restraint where no one takes risks and nothing bold gets done. This will damage the responsibility that your team feels, which will damage your **A-B-C Delegation.**

Big dreams and bold goals come with risks. When a strong effort falls short, don't bury it or lash out. Review it, learn from it, and demand that your team do the same.

A failure you learn from isn't a failure, but a failure you repeat or refuse to examine, is.

Encourage accountability, but also growth. True responsibility and true **A-B-C Delegation** include reflection, learning, and the courage to try again, but smarter.

Prepare for the Future

In high-performing teams, people aren't just completing tasks, they're responding to challenges, adapting to change, anticipating future needs, and responding to a changing world around them.

Responsiveness shouldn't be purely reactive and anchored in the present. It also means thinking ahead. Identifying a future issue and acting on it today is just as critical as addressing what's in front of you now. That kind of proactive engagement is a sign of deep ownership and it should be your goal for every team member. Responding to opportunity is as important as responding to everyday reality.

If your employees are only doing what they're told, you haven't truly delegated to them. You're not using **A-B-C Delegation** the way it's meant to function.

In conversations with your team, ensure that discussions on ownership are at least as frequent as discussions about tasks.

HOW TO SAY IT:
Cultivating Responsibility

Starter Lines: Set the tone for reflection, growth, and leadership mindset:

- "Let's talk about how you're showing ownership, not just execution."
- "Responsibility isn't about tasks, it's about how you respond to challenges."
- "I want you thinking like an owner of your Mandate Frame, not just a task-doer."

1. Mentoring Approach

Supportive, reflective tone

- "You've taken on a lot. How are you feeling about your scope of responsibility?"
- "Mistakes are part of growth. What matters is what we learn from them."
- "When you think about your Mandate Frame, what areas do you feel most connected to? And least connected to?"

2. Firm Approach

Standards-driven, growth-enabling tone

- "You own this part of the mission. I need you to treat it like it's yours."
- "Responsibility means anticipating challenges, not waiting for them to hit."
- "I expect you to reflect on how your work connects to the broader goals, not just your immediate tasks."

3. Tough Approach

High-stakes, accountability-centered tone

- "Right now, you're acting like a task manager. That's not enough. This role requires ownership."
- "Avoiding mistakes by avoiding responsibility is not leadership."
- "If you can't take initiative and lead your team, you're not the right person for this."

Closing Lines: End with challenge and support:

- "I want to see you own your role fully. Let's talk again in two weeks and assess your progress."
- "This is your opportunity to lead, not just deliver. Show me you're ready."
- "Step up, think long-term, and own it."

Takeaway: Responsibility is key to leadership. Use mentoring to develop it, firmness to expect it, and toughness when accountability must be enforced.

Example:

Cultivating Responsibility

Characters:

- Naomi (Senior Program Director)
- Samuel (Regional Field Manager)

Background:

Samuel led several field teams. He met deadlines and kept operations running, but when asked about long-term strategy or ownership, he deferred everything upward. His team waited for instructions instead of taking initiative. Naomi saw missed potential.

The Conversation:

Naomi: "Samuel, you've done a solid job with execution. But I want to talk about leadership beyond just task management. I need you to own your Mandate Frame and help your team do the same."

Samuel: "I've focused on getting everything done right. I didn't want to overstep."

Naomi: "I appreciate the discipline. But A-B-C Delegation isn't about staying safe. It's about building trust and ownership. Right now, your team is hesitant because they don't feel empowered. You set the tone."

Samuel: "So you want me to give them more autonomy?"

Naomi: "Yes, and do it intentionally. Talk with them about what they own, where they can act, and when they should involve you. Mistakes might happen, but that's part of learning. You grew when I gave you space to lead. Now it's your turn to do the same."

Samuel: "Got it. I'll start by reviewing Mandate Frames with my leads and setting up A-B-C Check-ins."

Naomi: "Perfect. And reflect on your role, too. Don't just manage tasks. Model leadership. That's how we build a culture of responsibility."

Why It Worked:

- Naomi praised what was working, but raised the bar.
- She reframed leadership as empowerment, not control.
- Samuel left with clarity, accountability, and a next step.

Takeaway:

Responsibility doesn't grow by chance. It grows when leaders model ownership, invite it, and support it consistently.

Summary: Developing New Leaders

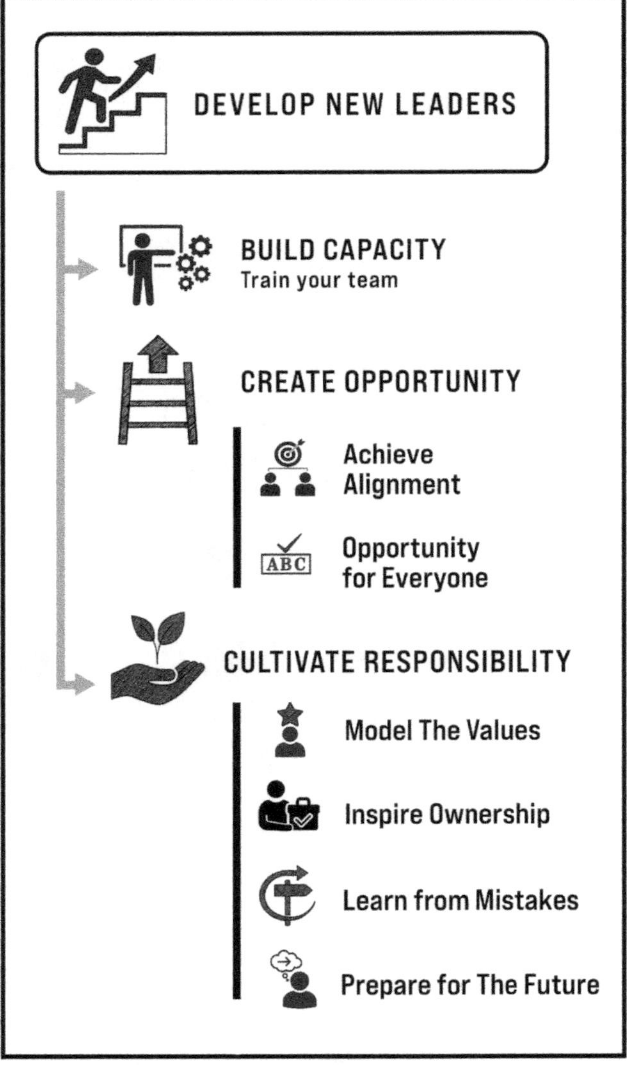

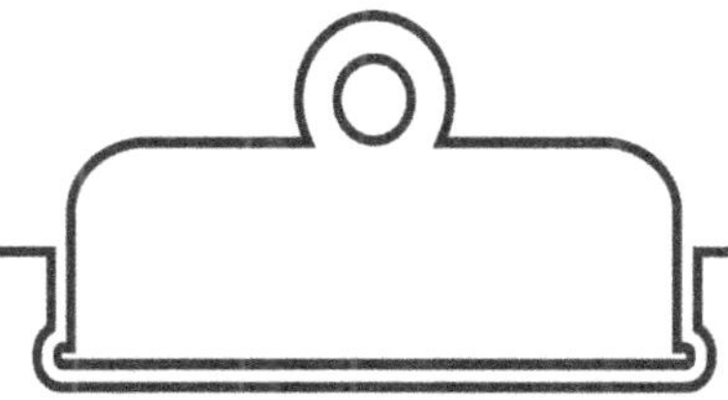

Requirement Three: Develop New Leaders

DO THIS TODAY

- ☐ Select one team member and move one task from Category C to B. Then tell them why.
- ☐ Outline one stretch opportunity for someone who's ready (e.g., lead a project, own a new area).
- ☐ Ask each direct report, "What are you hoping to grow into this year?"
- ☐ Review your own delegation habits. Are you giving real ownership or just more tasks?
- ☐ Identify one critical skill your team will need in the next 6 months. Then design a simple training or shadowing opportunity to build it now.

ASK YOURSELF:

WHAT IS YOUR DELEGATION STYLE?

Your delegation style reflects how you lead under pressure, how much you trust your team, and how well you connect tasks to purpose. Before implementing **A-B-C Delegation**, take an honest look at your current delegation habits, because self-awareness is the first step to improvement.

The ten most common styles of delegation

1. The Helicopter

You assign a task, but then stay too close. You question every decision and often step in before it's complete.

Problem: Your team feels micromanaged. You waste time on oversight instead of leadership.

Fix: Set expectations clearly, then step back. Let **Category A** and **Category B** tasks happen without interference, then follow up on them and evaluate them intentionally.

2. The Ghost

You delegate...and disappear. You assume no news is good news.

Problem: Your team lacks support and direction. Issues fester. Accountability weakens.

Fix: Check in regularly in the form of A-B-C Check-ins, and schedule evaluate. Visibility prevents drift and builds trust.

3. The Firefighter

You delegate reactively in moments of panic, without planning or clarity.

Problem: Chaos follows. The team gets dumped on, quality drops, and confidence erodes.

Fix: Delegate responsibility early. Clarity before urgency is the mark of strong leadership.

4. The One-Person Show

You do everything yourself because you believe it's faster or better.

Problem: You burn out. Your team stays underdeveloped and bottlenecks grow.

Fix: Share the work. Great leaders don't do it all. They build people who can.

5. The Shadow Manager

You assign tasks but don't trust your team. You check behind their backs or gather updates through others.

Problem: Trust breaks down. Your team feels spied on instead of supported.

Fix: Ask for visibility openly. A culture of transparency outperforms a culture of suspicion.

6. The Intimidator

You delegate by command, use pressure as motivation, and react to problems with anger or blame.

Problem: People might comply, but never commit. Fear stifles growth and initiative.

Fix: Lead with clarity, not control. Respect fuels better results than fear ever will.

7. The Lost Compass

You delegate tasks but lack a clear grasp of the mission yourself. Priorities shift, messages conflict, and your team feels unmoored.

Problem: Work loses meaning. Your team becomes busy, but not aligned.

Fix: Recenter on the mission. Delegation only works when everyone knows what they're working toward.

8. The Under-the-Rug Manager

You see conflict or dysfunction, but look away. You avoid the elephant in the room and difficult conversations, and hope problems resolve themselves.

Problem: Problems fester, morale suffers, and your silence becomes permission for mediocrity.

Fix: Confront conflict early. Delegation requires accountability, and that means addressing breakdowns when they happen.

9. The Know-It-All

You delegate tasks, but don't listen to ideas. In fact, you listen poorly overall, and override suggestions with your own.

Problem: Your team disengages. Innovation dies. People do what you say but stop thinking for themselves.

Fix: Ask for input and listen to input. Great leaders build smarter teams by being smart enough to listen.

And finally…

10. The A-B-C Manager

Truly empowered, you delegate with clarity, follow up with intention, and stay anchored to the mission. You trust your people, and they trust you.

Result: Ownership grows. Collaboration thrives. You lead with scale and strength.

Awareness Before Change

Effective delegation begins with self-awareness. Every manager falls into unhelpful patterns, especially under pressure, but with reflection and intention you can shift from control to clarity, from silence to support, and from bottlenecks to breakthroughs.

Take the evaluation now to understand your current delegation blind spots and to understand the practical steps that you need to take to become an empowered **A-B-C Manager.**

Find the evaluation at:

www.abcdelegation.com/evaluation

The **A-B-C Delegation** model gives you structure. An evaluation of your strengths and weaknesses will be a mirror. Use both. Your mission is too important for you to try to achieve it on your own.

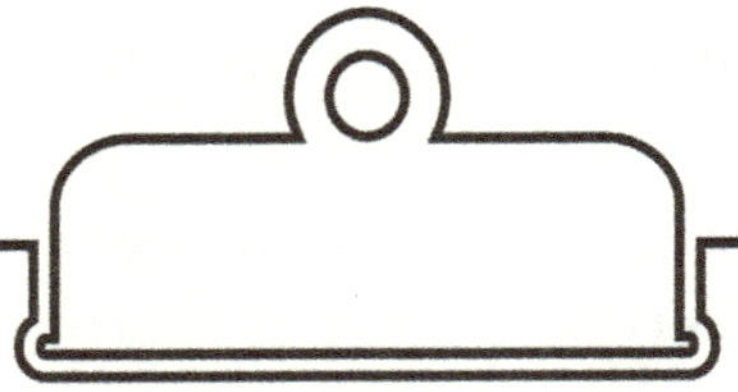

Committing to the Process

DO THIS TODAY

- ☐ Take the "What's Your Delegation Style?" quiz at abcdelegation.com/evaluation.
- ☐ Discover your top delegation blind spot (e.g., micromanaging, disappearing) and name it aloud.
- ☐ Share one insight from this book with a peer or fellow manager.
- ☐ Start a tracker: List your team's Mandate Frames and one action to grow each person.
- ☐ Write a short leadership commitment statement. What will change in how you lead?

BUILDING YOUR DELEGATION CULTURE

A-B-C Delegation is more than a method. It's a culture.

Effective delegation doesn't end with one check-in, one system rollout, or one successful project. *True leadership builds systems that outlast the leader.*

When your entire team understands the boundaries of ownership, follows a shared structure for communication, and grows through responsibility, it is a team that can truly excel and grow.

What a Delegation Culture Looks Like

In a healthy delegation culture:

- Mandate Frames are known, respected, and reviewed regularly.
- A-B-C categorization is second nature. It's not debated, but instinctive.
- Check-ins aren't interruptions. They're instruments of clarity and connection.
- Conflict is addressed early, with professionalism and mission-focus.
- Every manager builds leaders, not just workers.

This kind of culture increases speed, trust, accountability, and innovation. It removes guesswork and turns managers into multipliers.

Your Role as Culture Carrier

As a leader, you are not just implementing a framework, you are modeling the mindset behind it. That means:

- Delegating with clarity.
- Following up with consistency.
- Addressing breakdowns with courage.
- Investing in growth, even when it slows you down today to speed the team up tomorrow.

If you do this well, others will follow. Your team will replicate your behavior and middle managers will empower their teams the same way you empowered them.

Always remind yourself that the culture will only be cultivated if you model it.

What to Do Now

To build a delegation culture that lasts, focus on these five habits:

1. **Mandate Mastery**
   Review Mandate Frames with your team quarterly. Adjust as roles evolve, and make ownership visible.

2. **Structured Conversations**
   Keep A-B-C Check-ins short, focused, and regular.

3. **Model Judgment**
   Share your reasoning on A-B-C calls. Let your team learn *how you think*, not just *what you do*.

4. **Grow Leaders at Every Level**
   Give real authority, not just more tasks. Move tasks from C → B, and B → A, to let people stretch.

5. **Reinforce with Recognition**
   Celebrate responsible ownership. Recognize initiative and make it clear what good delegation looks like in action.

The Long View

If you lead with clarity, follow up with consistency, resolve conflict quickly, and develop your people intentionally, you'll create a team and a workplace where delegation is not feared, but expected. And you will develop a team where delegation is not just practiced, but perfected.

And that's when your leadership truly multiplies.

**"Don't just delegate.
Build a culture that does."**

**It's how you lead without
micromanaging, and without losing control.**

Need support in your team's transition to A-B-C Delegation?

Do you want a workshop or a training session for your leadership team? Do you need help rolling out **A-B-C Delegation** across your organization? Do you want materials to support you in your transition to effective delegation?

For online resources and
a full list of our services, please see
www.abcdelegation.com
or contact us at **info@abcdelegation.com.**

About the Author

Stefan has over two decades of leadership experience, primarily in humanitarian work.

His work earned recognition from Oprah Winfrey when she named him to her inaugural *SuperSoul 100* list, a group of 100 "awakened leaders" using their gifts and voices to help elevate humanity.

Though originally headed for a career in finance, a year of volunteer service in Central America transformed both his direction and purpose. Since then, Stefan has led humanitarian programs across Honduras, Peru, and the United States, often in high-stakes environments shaped by poverty, violence, and migration. In these roles, he has overseen teams ranging from a few hundred staff members to more than four thousand. He has served in both nonprofit and private-sector organizations, always focused on practical, high-impact leadership.

The **A-B-C Delegation** framework presented in this book is the product of that experience. It's not theoretical, but a proven system that Stefan has seen work with empirically trained aid workers and Ivy League–educated executives alike, by improving leadership and clarity.

Stefan was born in Washington, D.C., raised in Luxembourg, educated in England and Germany, and has spent over fifteen years of his career working in Latin America. He brings a truly global perspective to leadership and service. He holds a Bachelor of Science in Economics from the University of Warwick and a Master of Science in Development Administration and Planning from University College London (UCL).

Stefan believes **A-B-C Delegation** is, at its core, a practical tool. It helps managers define and clearly communicate when they need to be asked, when they want to be informed, and when they're happy to stay out of the way. This simple system has given Stefan a shared language to empower his teams and a structure to hold them accountable, enabling him to delegate without micromanaging and lead without losing control.

A-B-C Delegation has transformed the way Stefan leads. He wants it to do the same for you.